Red's Bed

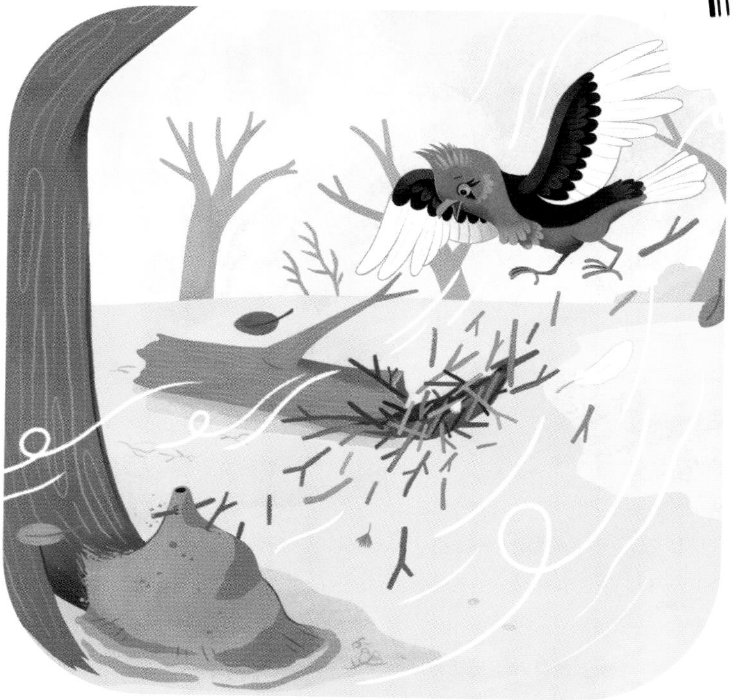

Written by Tanya Luther

Illustrated by Kristen Humphrey

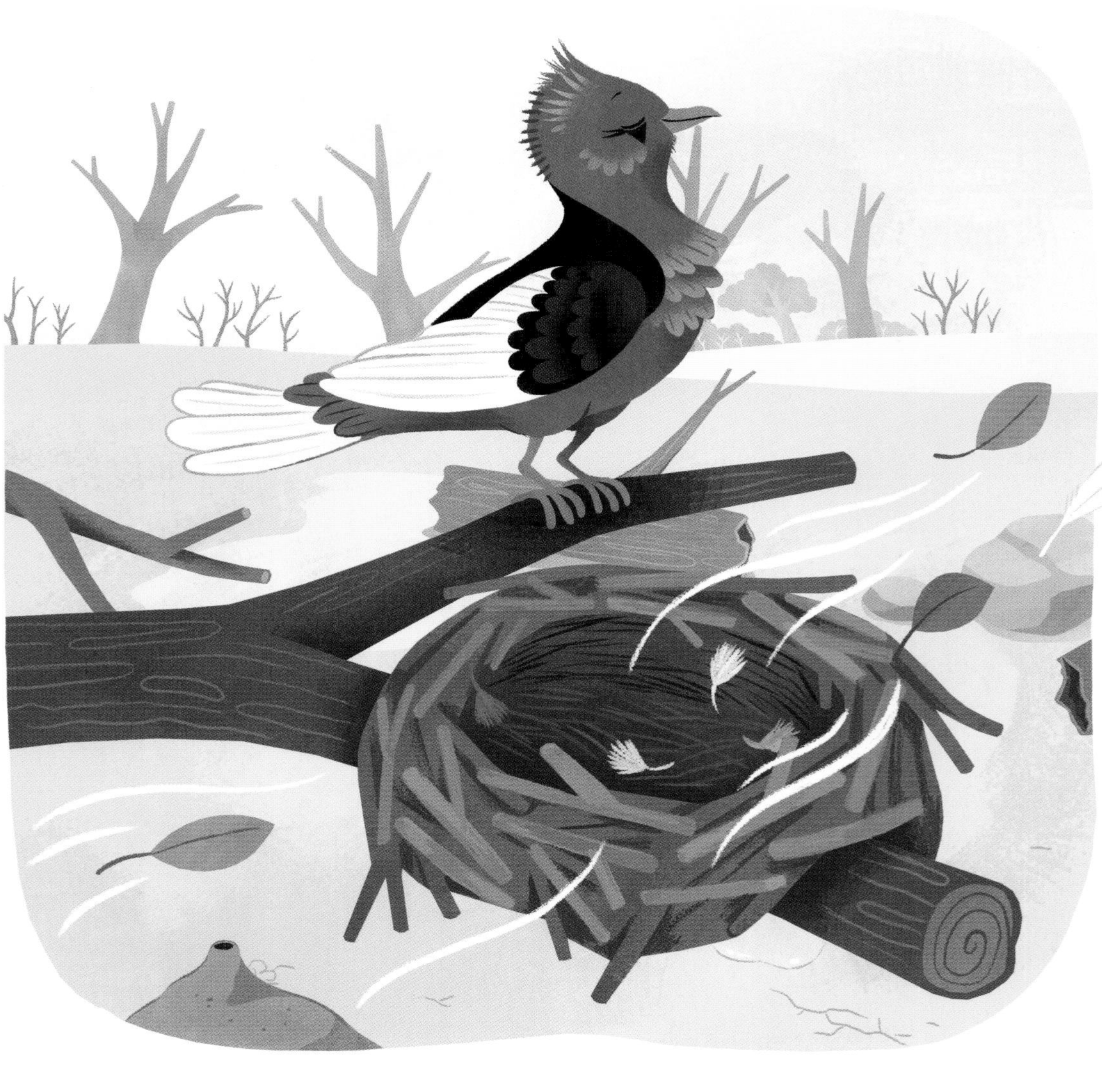

Red has a big bed. It is fab!

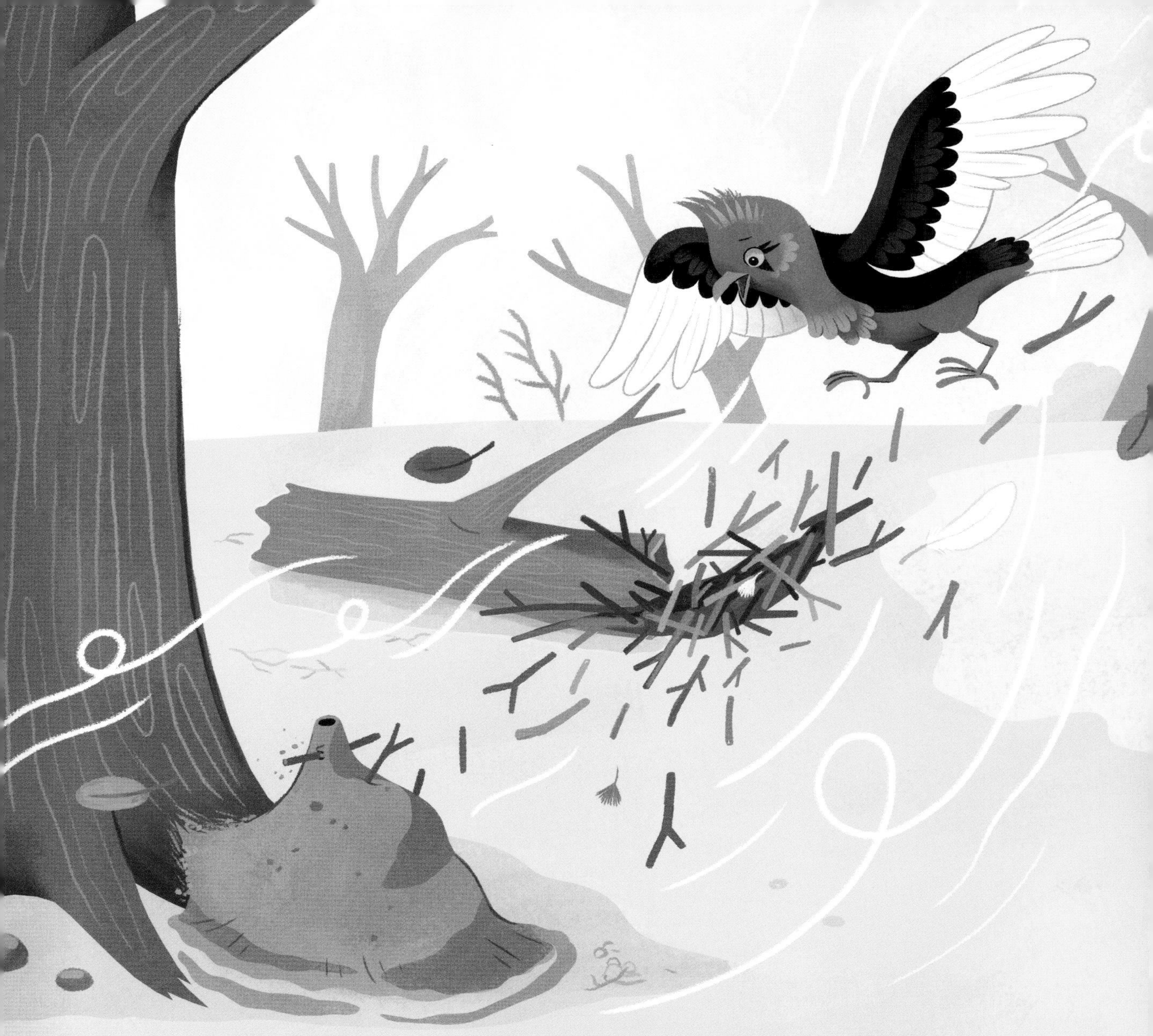

No! Red's bed is a mess!

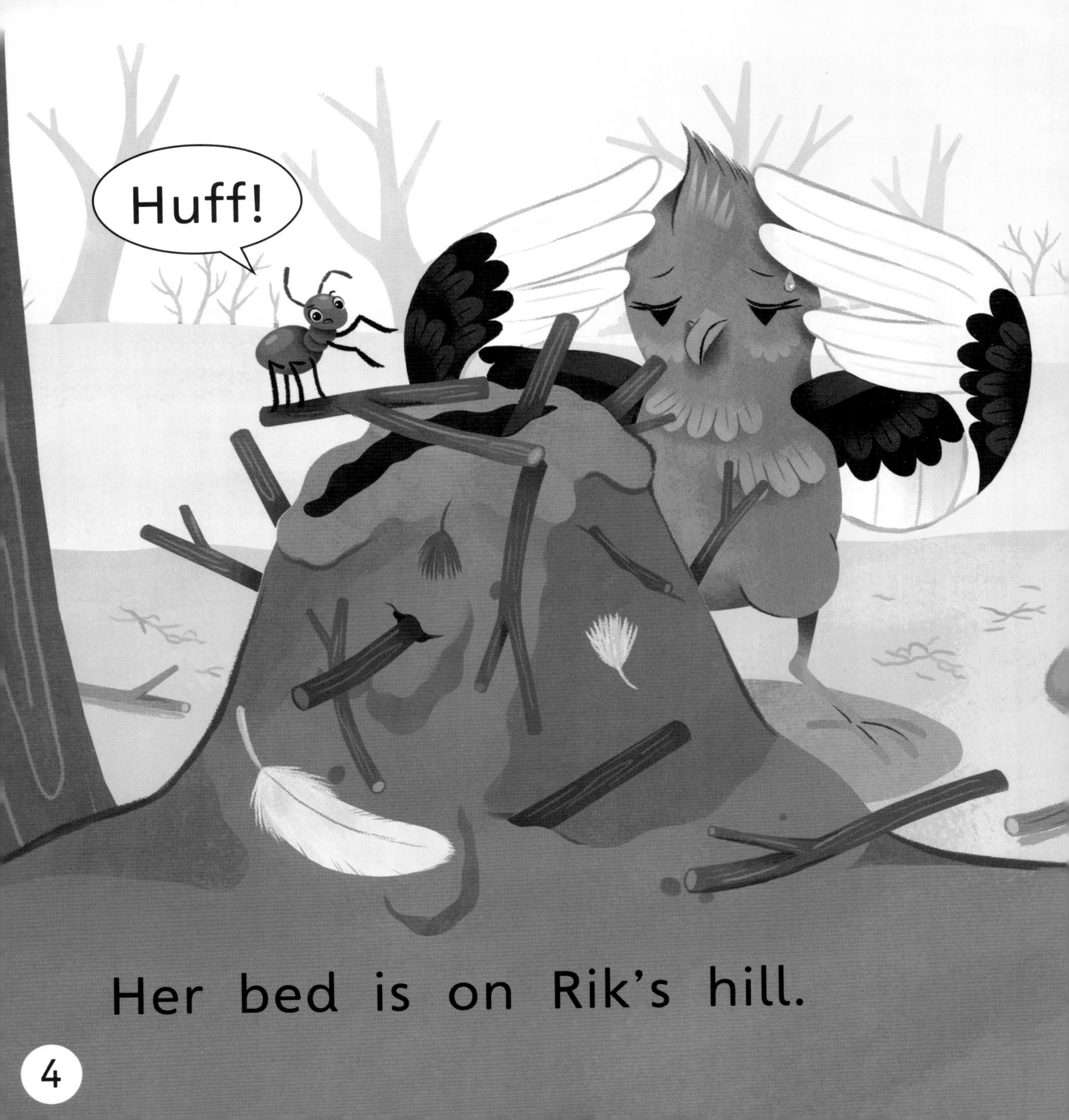

Her bed is on Rik's hill.

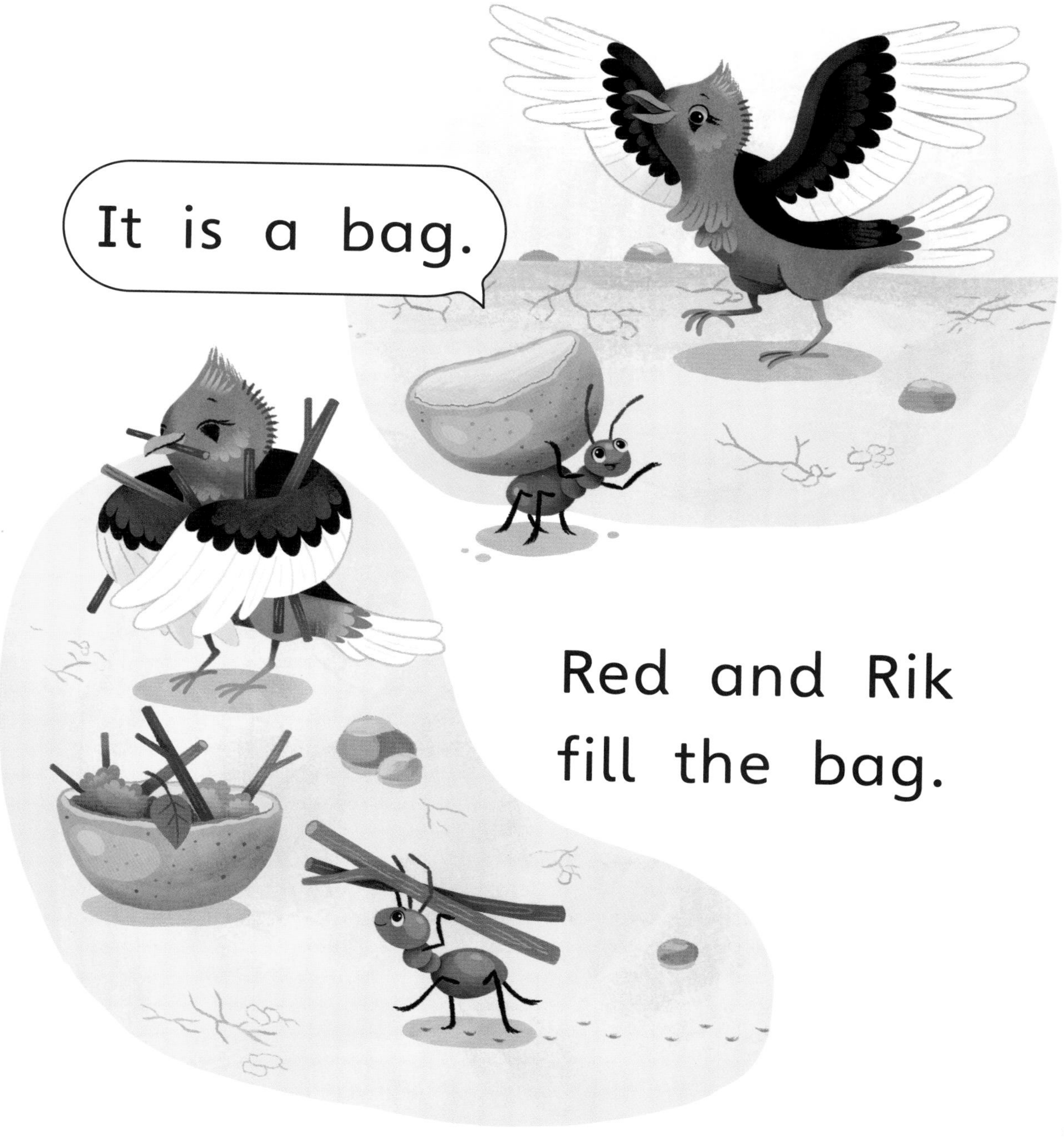

Red and Rik
fill the bag.

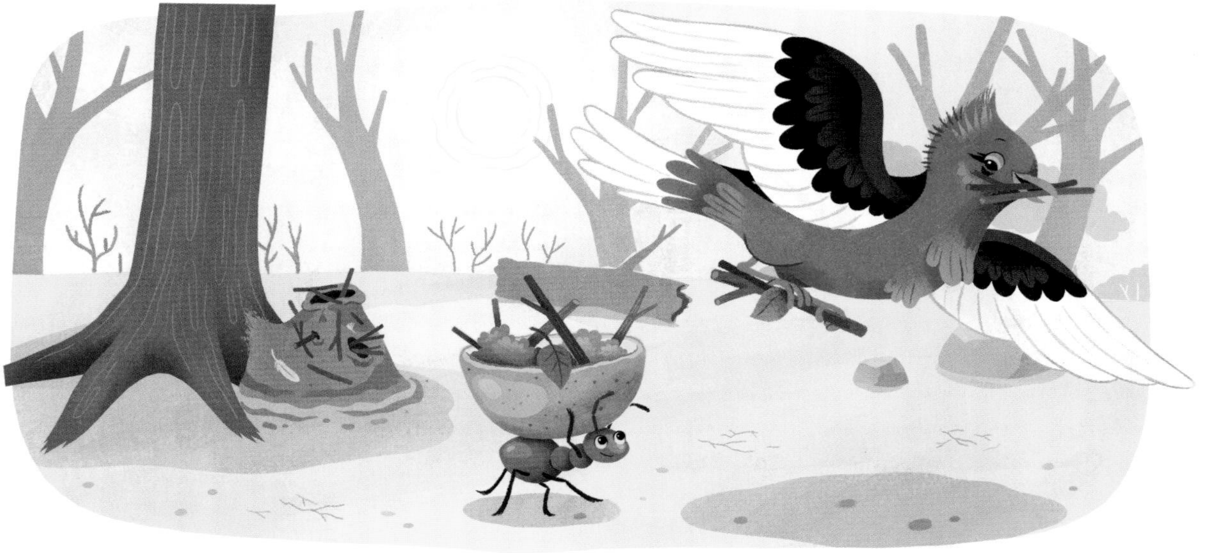

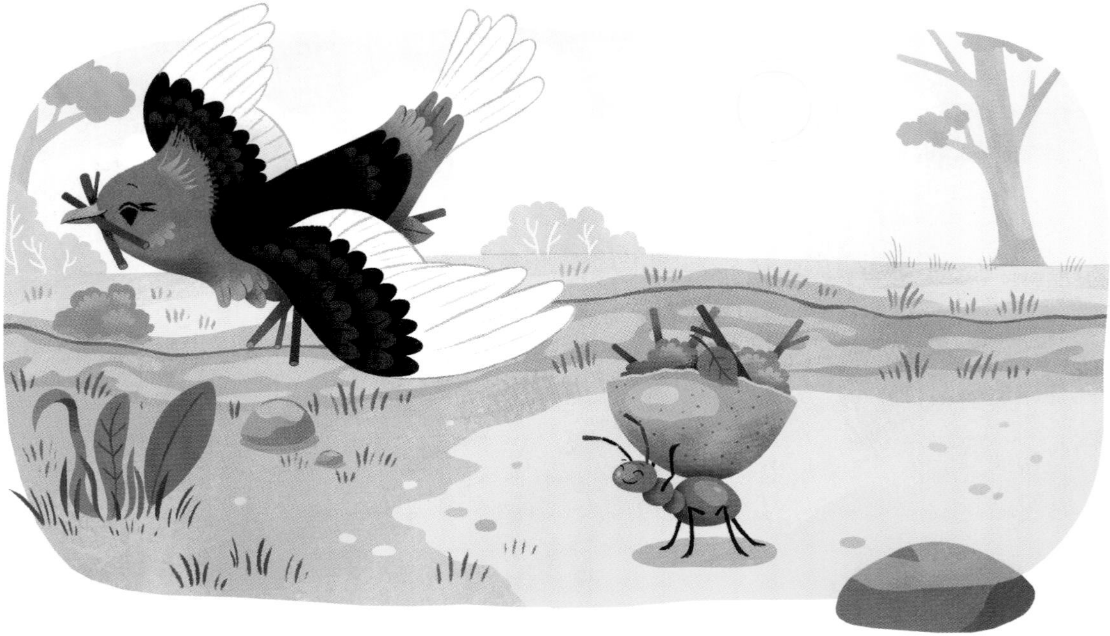

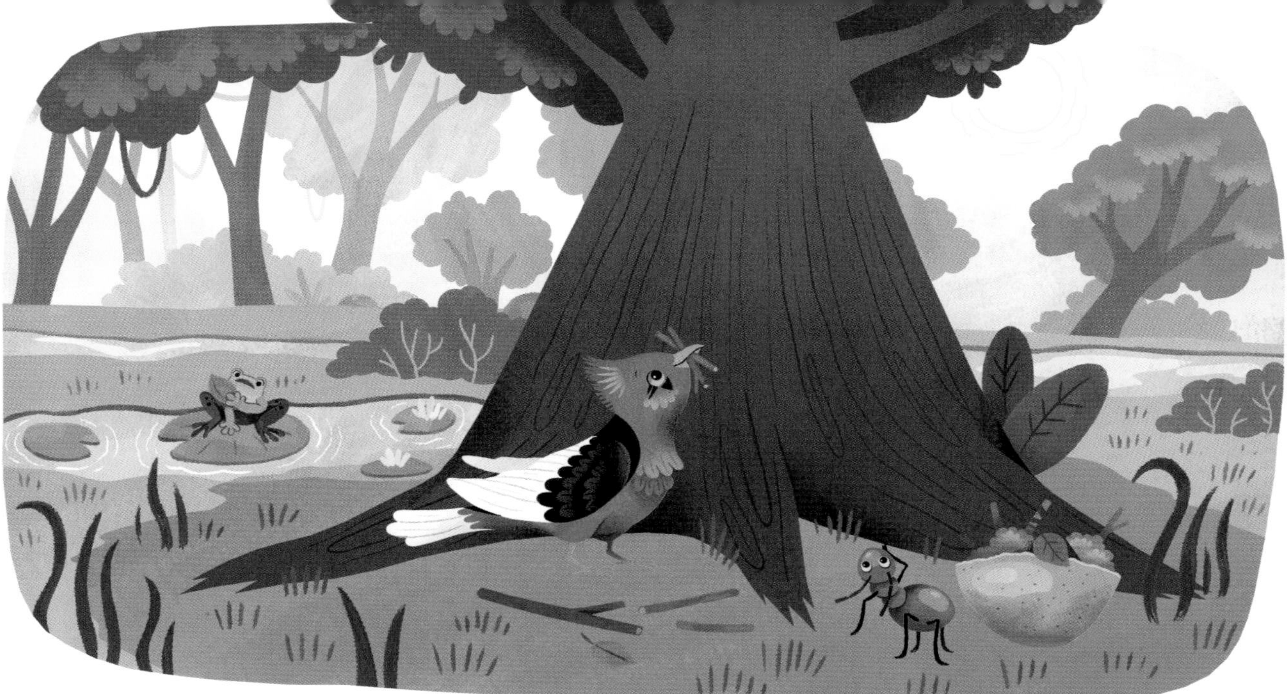

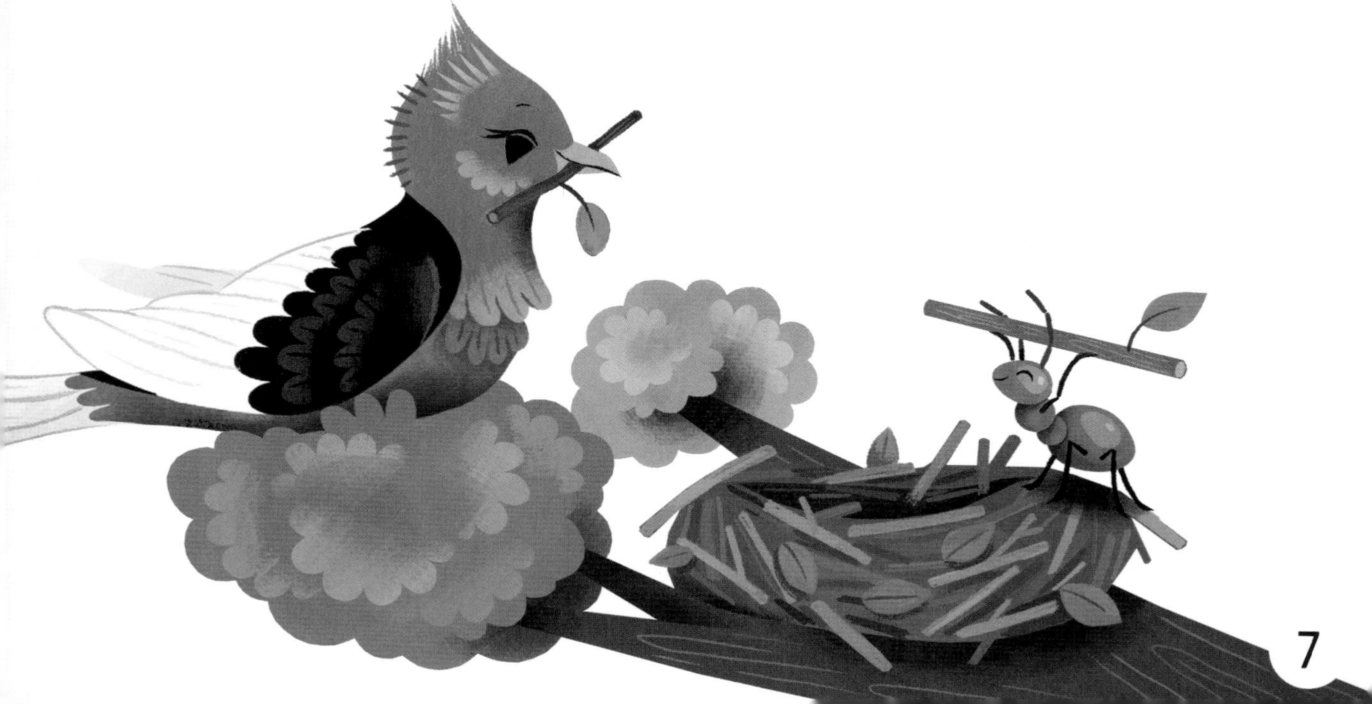

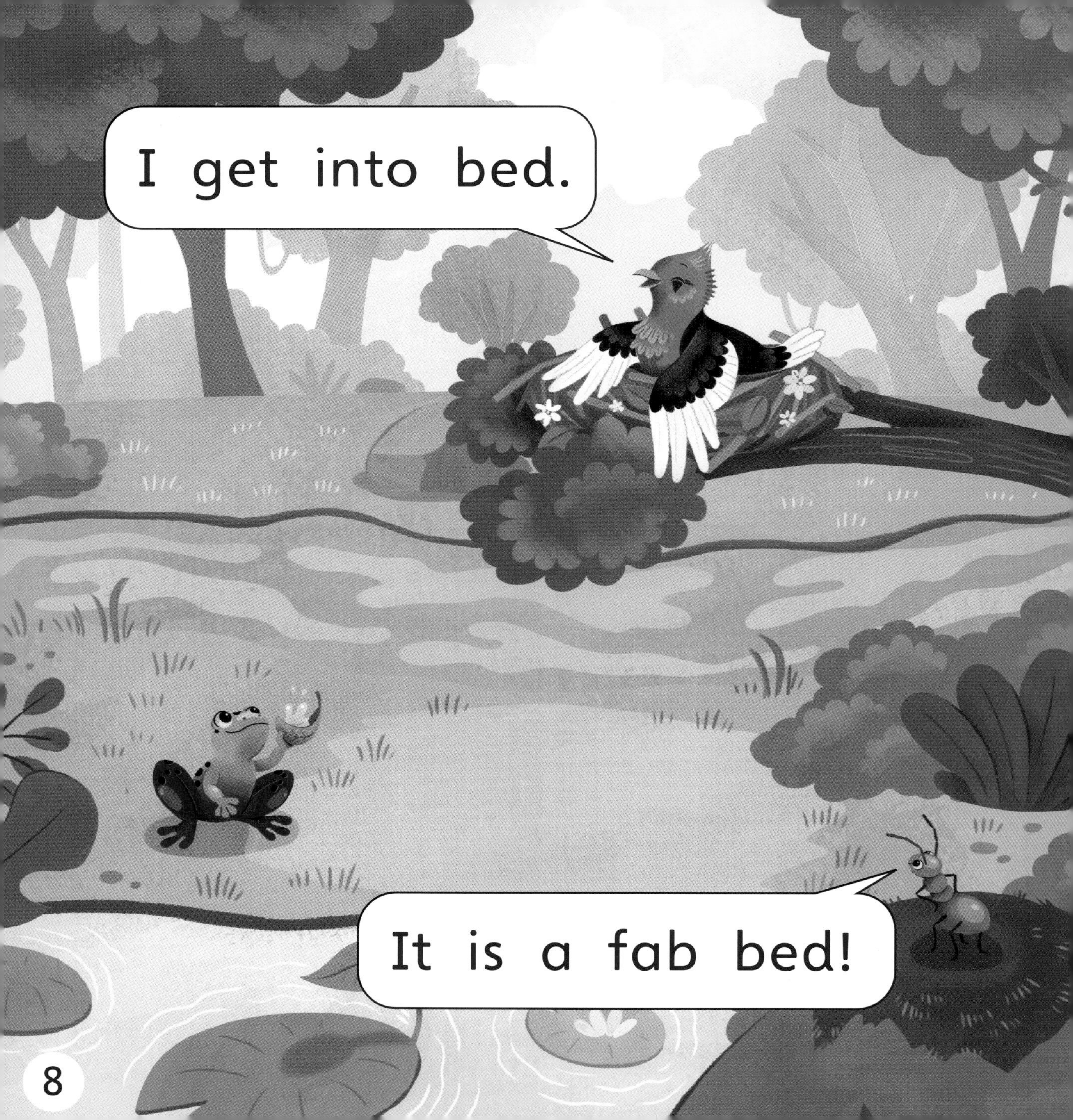
I get into bed.
It is a fab bed!